ALSO BY LUC

About (
A Practical Guide to Bri

'I really enjoyed reading this both as a mother and as a child psychologist. The examples flowed off the page to reinforce the points beautifully.'

Julie Stokes, OBE, Founder of Winston's Wish

'A brilliant read! ... How does she know this, is she a man?'

Phil Hood, Youth Worker

'Everyone needs to read this book in order to get a full understanding on how us males tick.'

Tony Thompson, Boyz 2 Men Project

Bringing the Best out in Boys
Communication Strategies for Teachers

'Will certainly make teachers think, and be alert to what's different about teaching boys, and how to make this more of a pleasure.'

Steve Biddulph, author of *Manhood* and *Raising Boys*

'Lucinda Neall's wise book ... is one of the most interesting accounts available of an over-familiar issue, distinguished by its practical approach.'

Times Educational Supplement

'I can honestly say this is the book that has done most to change my work as a teacher. Everyone should be made to read this as part of ongoing CPD!'

'Inspired Teacher' from Norfolk - *Amazon Review*

Lucinda Neall

How to Talk to Teenagers

Leaping Boy Publications

How to Talk to Teenagers
2013 edition

Published by Leaping Boy Publications
tel: 0044 (0) 1525 222 600
email: partners@neallscott.co.uk
www.howtotalktoteenagers.com

Cover design and typesetting by Deborah Hawkins
Cover illustrations by Conor Neall and
Guerrilla Digital Media

Printed and distributed by Lightning Source UK Ltd
British Library Cataloguing in Publication Data
applied for

ISBN 978-0-9926464-0-0

With thanks to my parents
who set me on my path

Contents

Introduction

This book is designed to be an easy reference book for anyone involved with teenagers. It gives tips and strategies on how to communicate with them in ways that encourage co-operation and a positive attitude.

It is full of real-life examples that are drawn from the home, the street, the outdoors, clubs, sport and school. The principles outlined in it are adaptable to any setting.

How to Use the Book

The book is divided into three parts: the first covers some basics of how to get on with teenagers; the second gives you particular strategies that set everyone up to win; the third looks at how to sort things out when they are going wrong, how to talk about alcohol, sex and drugs, and how to involve teenagers in the community. There is a two-page summary at the back.

If you have time, read the whole book quickly to get a feel for what's in it. If you don't, look at Part I, then skim through the rest, picking up on the advice boxes and the two-page summary.

When you have a particular problem use the contents page to find the section that will help. If it feels like you are having a constant battle with a teenager, you might look at 'How to Stop Nagging and Shouting' or 'Avoiding Conflict and Arguments'. If someone is lacking in confidence, read the section on 'Building Self-Esteem'.

If you've tried all the strategies in Part II and it still isn't working, then look at Part III, which covers Problem Solving.

You might want to set up a group who meet regularly and choose a particular section to cover each time. The sections on 'Maintaining Boundaries' and 'Giving Feedback' are particularly useful for parents.

The book can also be used for training people who work with teenagers. The section headings, advice boxes and summary can give pointers for training topics.

PART I

Getting the Basics Right

Understanding Their World

It's funny how easily many adults forget what they were like as adolescents. Think back – how was it for you? Hormones racing, obsessed with the latest fashion, what you looked like and what your peers thought of you? A rebel, pushing boundaries, experimenting with everything you could? Concerned about the future, feeling let down by the previous generation, convinced you could do a better job?

Remember what it's like to be a teenager

Today's teenagers are not so different. If we can put ourselves in their shoes, try to see the world from their point of view and understand their priorities and concerns; then a dialogue between the generations can begin.

When an adult can see the world through young eyes, it can reap surprisingly positive responses.

A man walking along the pavement saw three boys on BMX bikes; he did not know them. One had been jumping over a milk bottle and left it rolling on the pavement as they rode off.

'Excuse me,' the man called. On the second call the boy stopped and turned round. 'I'm seriously impressed by those jumps,' the man said, 'but I don't want anyone walking by to trip over the milk bottle. Can you put it back where you found it?'
'I'm sorry!' responded the boy and returned the milk bottle to the doorstep.

Some teenagers were hanging around in the dark near a youth club. An adult who occasionally helped at the club saw them as she walked past.
'Hi there,' she said, 'I don't recognise you in the dark, are you part of the youth club?' No, they weren't.
'OK,' she continued, 'I'm just going there now,' and carried on. As she rounded the corner a voice called out after her: 'Nice to meet you!'

In these examples the adult sees the world through the eyes of the young people – they are having fun. From the their point of view what they are doing is harmless; but from some adults' point of view the teenagers in the dark may appear threatening, and the boys on their bikes could seem like vandals. Such perceptions risk becoming self-fulfilling. If young people are feared and no one engages with them, they become isolated and operate by their own rules. If they are confronted without understanding, they feel aggrieved and respond rudely. Recognising their view of the world makes it easier for them to co-operate.

Making That Connection

If you know and like a young person, it's relatively easy to use that relationship to ask them to do or not do something. You know where they are coming from, so you see and appeal to the best in them. But if you don't know them, it's easy to make judgments, assume the worst and treat them accordingly. This often results in a bad reaction from the young person and a bad relationship from the start.

It's worth making a conscious effort to build a relationship with young people that will provide a foundation for future interactions.

Make a habit of being friendly to youngsters. Smile and say hello. Learn what their interests and hobbies are so you have something to make small talk about. Find out what teams they support or what pets they have.

Make a point of saying something positive

Many young people are used to being ignored by adults unless there is something negative to say. Surprise them by saying something nice.

'You look as though you're having fun.'

'Thanks for scooping up the dog poop.'

'That's an amazing trick. How do you do that?'

'Nice haircut, Tim.'

The more positive contact you have with a young person – the more they know, like and respect you – the easier it will be in the future if things get tricky. If you've known someone since they were young and you come across them doing something stupid as a teenager, when you ask them to stop they probably will. If it's the first time you've ever spoken to them, the situation is likely to be far more difficult.

Listening

A good way to get into the shoes of the young is to listen to what they say. As adults we often demand young people listen to us, but may not be very good at listening to them.

If we listen and seek to understand where they are coming from, then half the work is done: not only will they feel respected and that their views matter, but they will also be willing to listen to us.

> **If you listen to them
> they will listen to you**

Acknowledgement

We can make sure young people know we have heard and understood them by acknowledging what they say.

Acknowledgment does not necessarily mean you agree with the other person or condone their behaviour; it simply shows you are listening and trying to understand. If a young person feels heard and understood, then he or she is likely to give respect and co-operation in return.

Hearing their reality is more important than trying to come up with a solution for them.

Boy: *'I'm bored. There's nothing to do in this stupid place!'*
Adult: 'Life's not much fun when you feel bored.'

In fact acknowledgment can help a teenager sort out a problem on their own.

Girl: *'Kylie's a bitch!'*
Adult: 'Oh?'
Girl: *'She sent me a text saying ... !'*
Adult: 'I see.'
Girl: *'OK, so yesterday I did ...'*
Adult: 'Mmmm.'
Girl: *'I think I'll ...(explain/make friends).'*
Adult: 'Right.'

Acknowledging what you think you've heard can help formulate your understanding.

'So you're worried that everyone else will be allowed to go to the party except you?'

Acknowledgment can also take you a long way when young people seem to be behaving unreasonably.

A music festival has been organised in the park and as a result the skateboarding area is out of use for the day; a notice about it has been up for weeks. Whilst most young people are pleased to have a festival, the skateboarders and BMX riders are unhappy. They gather outside the skate park, complaining that their facility has been taken away.

Instead of: 'I don't know what you're complaining about. It's only one day out of 365, and you had loads of notice. You should consider yourselves lucky to live in a town that has a skate park and a music festival.'

say: 'I can see you're really annoyed that you can't use the skate park for a whole day. I don't think anyone realised how much you'd all mind. When we organise next year's festival it would be really good if you came along to say what you think and helped us come up with a better way of doing it.'

It is easy to interpret young people's sense of mischief or adventure as anti-social, but if you can get where they are coming from, you can help them understand how others see the world.

Instead of: 'There is nothing funny about "knock and run"! You were victimising that old lady. Next time you do anything like that you'll be reported to the police!'

say: 'I can see that it might seem funny, her coming to the door and no one being there. However, look at it from her point of view. She's got arthritis and even walking to the front door is painful. No wonder she gets angry when there's no one there!'

Instead of: 'Mr Jones told me he caught you and your friends lighting a fire on the waste ground. You know fires are dangerous. Why did you do such a stupid thing?'

say: 'I know fires are fascinating, but you are not to light them up there. Let's make a fire pit in the yard; then you'll be able to have a fire without upsetting other people.'

One way to get an angle on where young people are coming from is to ask them.

'I'm really not keen on those lyrics. What is it you like about them?'

Listening to young people's views can be very enlightening. I once went to the school council at a local upper school to ask them what they'd like to see done to improve the town. I was expecting them to ask for more and better facilities for their age group. Instead they said that the thing that would make the most difference to them was a Saturday police patrol on the High Street. It turned out that there was a small group of teenagers who took pocket money off other kids each weekend. There was no police presence to inhibit them and no one dared report them for fear of getting beaten up. I'm pleased to say there is now a regular police presence in the town.

- **See the world through teenagers' eyes**

- **Find out what they are interested in**

- **Listen to their point of view**

- **Seek their opinions**

- **Acknowledge their reality**

Imparting Values

One of the jobs of an adult is to teach the younger generation values. The best way to pass values onto the next generation is to be an example of them.

If youngsters are around adults who are respectful, caring, courteous and honest, then they are likely to copy their behaviour and take on their values. If they see disrespect, dishonesty, selfishness or materialism, these are the values they are likely to take on.

Values are caught not taught

Even when there are bad influences in other areas of their lives, when young people respect and admire a particular adult, they tend to emulate their behaviour and values.

Consciously or subconsciously, teenagers look at adults in their lives as models of manhood and womanhood. Not just parents or celebrities, but all the adults they come across. Each one of us gives them a possible model to choose.

Teenagers do not respond well to lectures, but we can still make values clear by what we say.

'Let's put the litter in the bin.'

'They look like they could do with some help.'

'I'm not prepared to lie about your age.'

'I was wrong. I'm sorry.'

'We don't have name-calling in this group.'

'It takes courage to stand up for someone who is being picked on.'

Values will be conveyed through the way we talk about our lives, our work and other people, through the opinions we express and the anecdotes we tell. And young people learn as much from what we do as from what we say. If they see their parents being affectionate, they'll learn about love; if they hear adults speaking respectfully to each other, they'll understand respect; if they are around people who are polite to one another, then courtesy will come more naturally to them.

We can reinforce the values we want by noticing when teenagers put them into practice.

'Thanks for letting me by.'

'That was very helpful.'

'Well done for staying calm when he said that.'

Encourage young people to have respect for themselves and each other.

'You're better than that.'

'Hey, that's not very nice, there's no need to swear.'

'I don't like hearing you talk about the opposite sex like that.'

Some adults believe that respect should be earned and only given to those they deem worthy of it. Many young people agree with this view. Unfortunately it results in a stalemate: an adult won't show respect to a young person because he or she is not respectful or respect-worthy; the young person won't show respect to the adult because he or she does not seem respectful or respect-worthy.

If we want the next generation to be respectful, we have to teach them by example, treating them with the respect we would like them to show to others.

- **Live your values**

- **Don't give lectures**

- **Acknowledge what young people do right**

- **Show respect in what you do and say**

Body Language

Analysis by body language expert Alan Pease showed that 60-80% of a person's impact can be as a result of their body language and vocal tone. So, whilst the words we use are important, we must be aware of our body language and tone of voice to understand our full impact.

The difficulty with body language, and particularly facial expressions, is that we are on the inside looking out, so we are often unaware of what we are doing. Yet everything gives a message: how close you are, whether you are physically on the same level, the stance you take up, the position of your hands and how you hold them, whether you smile or frown, whether your eyes twinkle or glare.

> **Ask for feedback from someone you trust**

Find out what habits you have and their impact. Once you become aware of your body language, you will find it easier to choose the impact you want.

Tone of Voice

Your tone of voice is easier to be aware of since you can hear it, but it may still be helpful to get feedback from others.

Listen to yourself when you speak to teenagers. When you ask them to do something, do you sound firm and respectful? If not, what could you do differently to achieve that? Do you need to change the volume, pitch, speed, tone or emphasis?

Young people pick up on whether you appear to mean what you say; if you don't seem to, they pay little attention. Try taking a deeper breath before you speak: this lowers the pitch, which gives the voice more authority, and helps you relax, reducing any sense of stress.

The youth worker went into the hall and saw sweet papers all over the floor. She held out the bin in front of her and called out above the noise, 'Everyone put five pieces of litter in the bin!' Her tone was friendly but purposeful and she kept repeating the request until everyone got the message. Three minutes later the floor was clean.

Watch out that your voice doesn't sound like it's pleading. Try delivering questions without the voice going up at the end, so they sound like statements instead of requests.

Instead of: 'Can I have your attention?'
say: 'Can I have your attention.'

Occasionally an angry tone can be effective, giving young people the message that they have seriously overstepped the mark. But if adults frequently sound angry, young people stop taking any notice.

Injecting some lightness or humour into your delivery can sometimes be all that's needed to get co-operation.

- **Be aware of the messages you give with your body, voice, face and eyes**

- **Adopt tones, gestures and facial expressions that are firm, non-threatening and respectful**

- **Taking a deep breath relaxes the body and lowers the voice**

Humour

Young people like to have a laugh and a joke, and a good way to build a better relationship with them is through humour. Humour is a personal thing and what works will depend on your style and the particular situation. Used well, it can lighten the atmosphere and aid co-operation.

The youth worker has put some new posters up at different angles round the walls. Wanting a bit of attention, some teenagers start taking them down. Tongue in cheek, the youth worker says, 'Do you realise I've spent the whole afternoon putting those up with a spirit level?'
The teenagers mock the angles of the posters, and others join in the laughter. With a straight face the youth worker says, 'I'm sure you couldn't do any better!'
The young people rise to the challenge by putting up the posters they have taken down and repositioning all the others.

The purpose of using humour is to makes things easier, so don't use it to put young people down. Instead, make a joke of the situation or of yourself.

Two teenage boys are play fighting and don't stop when asked to. One is bigger and stronger than the other, and has overpowered him. A group has gathered round to watch. The adult says to the smaller boy: 'Hey, why do you always target the weak and vulnerable? I suppose you'll pick on me next!'

The boys stop fighting as everyone laughs.

Boys in particular enjoy banter and it can be a great way of getting on with teenagers. There is a very fine line between banter and sarcasm. Whilst sarcasm might raise a laugh, it can also wound, and victims may look for an opportunity to get their own back.

> **Take care with sarcasm**

However tough an exterior they present to the world, both girls and boys can be extremely sensitive, especially during adolescence. Make sure that everyone is able to enjoy the joke.

If adults exemplify playful constructive humour, this will rub off on young people. Of course they will overstep the mark sometimes, but part of an adult's job is to teach young people appropriateness and timing.

'Joking is fine, rudeness is not.'

'That kind of humour isn't appropriate in this company.'

However inappropriate their humour, the trick is not to take it personally, as it will only wind you up and make things worse. This is an especially useful strategy when teenagers are deliberately trying to wind you up.

A girl calls a police community support officer a 'plastic pig'.

Instead of getting angry or upset about it

say: 'Sounds like some kind of moneybox. Well, at least that makes me worth something!'

- **Use humour to lighten the atmosphere**

- **Laugh with teenagers not at them**

- **Don't take young people's joking personally**

PART II

Making It Easy for Yourself

Maintaining Boundaries

A boundary is the line between acceptable and unacceptable behaviour. Clear boundaries that are not too restrictive and are consistently enforced give young people clarity and make them feel safe and cared for.

Adolescence is a time of exploration and testing things out, so expect teenagers to test boundaries. Some will blatantly push against them, others will try and get round them without being noticed.

Young people not only need boundaries, they want them. Boundaries provide an external safety net and give them the excuse to say 'I can't do this, I'm not allowed to.'

At times young people are unconsciously begging adults to enforce boundaries. When teenagers say, 'Do I have to?' a simple 'Yes' is usually all that's needed. Then they can do what has been asked without feeling obliged to resist further.

Young people need to know the limits of acceptable behaviour and what sanctions apply if those limits are overstepped, so rules and sanctions should be clearly defined.

Positive Language

If boundaries are constantly expressed in the negative –
'No...' or 'Don't...' – young people can feel controlled
and constrained, and react by rebelling. Boundaries are
more effective when phrased positively.

'Everyone helps with the clearing up.'

'Be back by 9.00 p.m.'

'Ball games on the grass.'

'Use respectful language.'

*'Your friends are welcome to visit, but I expect them to
come and say hello when they arrive and goodbye and
thank you when they leave.'*

Occasionally a boundary needs to be stated in the
negative in order to be explicit.

'No spitting.'

Displaying rules prominently ensures they are absorbed
even if they are not consciously read. It also makes the
rules independent of the adult enforcing them, so young
people are less likely to take it personally when they are
reminded of one.

Many boundaries will be fixed, but some may be
negotiable; it helps if young people are told which is
which, and why.

Club members have asked if a boisterous game can be organised.

Adult: 'There are a lot of people here tonight and the atmosphere is a bit wild. I don't want to play that game in case someone gets hurt. We'll do it on a night when there are fewer people and it's calmer.'

If a boundary is perceived as unreasonable, it is unlikely to be abided by, and there will be argument when it is enforced. If a boundary is perceived as reasonable and is enforced in a reasonable way, then young people are likely to comply.

The nature of teenagers is that they will overstep boundaries, so adults should not take this personally, but simply remind them of the boundary with clear, positive and impersonal language.

Instead of: 'I'm sick to death of having to tell you to go to bed!'

say: 'Your bedtime is ten o'clock.'

Instead of: 'Stop being so selfish, Tracey. Give Amber a turn!'

say: 'Tracey, it's Amber's turn.'

Young people who are in the habit of swearing are often unaware of how often they do, and gently pointing it out usually elicits an apology. A swear word can be met with a quizzical look, a finger to the lips or the word 'language'.

It is all too easy to notice when boundaries are over-stepped and yet forget to acknowledge when they are abided by. Make sure you say something when things are going well.

'Thank you for taking turns, Tracey.'

'It's good to see you back at the time we agreed.'

'It's great that you get your homework done without a fuss.'

'I've noticed you've really reduced how much you swear here. Thank you.'

Fairness and Consistency

If a boundary is applied consistently, then it is seen as firm; but if it is applied inconsistently, young people will perceive it as flexible and worth testing at every opportunity. It is much better to have firm boundaries that are relaxed on special occasions, than flexible boundaries that are suddenly tightened up when the adult has had enough.

Every adult will have a slightly different view of what is and is not acceptable, so it is worth the adults discussing and agreeing boundaries to avoid confusion. Sometimes the boundaries will differ with different people or in different places: for example, a higher level of noise may be acceptable for one adult or situation than another.

When enforcing a boundary give young people a little time and space to take on what they have been asked to do and decide to do it for themselves. This is called 'take-up time'. If young people feel treated respectfully and given a little space, they are more likely to comply; if they feel controlled or mistrusted, they may become resentful, rude and unco-operative. Allowing take-up time also implies a degree of confidence that the young people will do what has been asked.

> **Teenagers need 'take-up time'**

Most young people respond pretty well if they think they have been fairly treated. If they feel unfairly treated they frequently become angry. If someone has a reputation for behaving badly, adults tend to watch them, so they get caught more often than their peers. They then react because they feel as though they are being picked on.

Girls and boys tend to push boundaries in different ways. Often a girl will subtly step outside a boundary and draw little attention. A boy, on the other hand, tends to be more 'in your face'. It is important that a boundary be seen to apply equally to both girls and boys.

Part of fairness is being seen not to hold a grudge, so adults should make a point of dropping the issue after it's been dealt with. They can say something that makes this clear.

'OK. I've told you what I feel about it, now let's move on.'

'That's that dealt with. [pause] Anyway, I'm pleased I ran into you because I heard you'd done well in the dance competition and I wanted to congratulate you.'

There will be occasions when fairness and consistency have to be overridden by doing what works best in particular circumstances. Adults must use their own judgment in such cases. It often works to explain your reasoning.

With a teenager who doesn't usually put much effort into schoolwork:

Teenager: 'I need some money for my haircut – will you give me some?'

Parent: 'Normally I would say your haircut will have to wait till you get next month's allowance. On this occasion I've been so impressed at the amount of effort you put into your school project work that I'll pay for it as a "well done".'

Sometimes a boundary may need to be changed or tightened up. Make sure this is clearly explained and everyone knows about it, otherwise there will be problems when it is implemented.

With each birthday, certain boundaries will be relaxed. The reasoning and conditions behind this relaxation need to be explained and there should be some room for negotiation. However, there will still be some boundaries beyond which you are not yet prepared to go.

'Please don't take this personally. I'm not saying I don't trust you to have an unsupervised party. What I'm saying is, I don't trust sixteen-year-olds to have an unsupervised party. However good your intentions, if some of your friends drink too much and get out of hand, you can't guarantee how they will behave. If you want a party you can have one, as long as you understand that an adult will be on hand.'

Sanctions

When boundaries are exceeded, then sanctions usually apply. The purpose of sanctions is not, as is often imagined, to punish, but to teach self-discipline and encourage social and moral behaviour in the future. Sanctions should be chosen with this in mind.

Sanctions should be fair, proportionate, appropriate to the circumstances, and applied consistently and respectfully.

In order that young people learn from the situation, the sanction should ideally be a consequence of the misdemeanour.

If he makes a mess, he clears it up.

If she is five minutes late, she comes in five minutes early next time.

If he breaks something, he apologises / mends it / pays for it.

If she doesn't put her clothes in the wash basket, they don't get washed.

If they spray graffiti on a wall, they make the wall good.

**Choose a sanction that is
a <u>consequence</u> of behaviour**

It sometimes takes more thought and supervision to apply 'consequences' than punishments, but it is worth the effort because of the lessons learned. And as the consequence itself teaches a lesson, there is no need for a lecture!

There are times when there is no immediate sanction given, but the consequence of an action becomes apparent in due course.

A teenager refuses to help unload the shopping, and then later asks for a lift.

Instead of: 'You just take, take, take! You won't help me when I ask, but as soon as you want a lift it's all smiles and niceness. I just feel taken for granted!'
say (calmly): 'You didn't feel like helping me out earlier. I don't feel like helping you out now.'

The consequence needs to take place soon after the action in order for the connection to be clear.

Many adults make the mistake of imposing sanctions for longer than is needed for the lesson to be learnt. If the punishment outweighs the crime, it will seem unjust and any initial remorse will quickly be replaced by resentment. The longer the sanction is in place, the more the resentment will grow, so instead of the punishment encouraging better behaviour, it can result in a stand-off and worse behaviour.

Instead of: 'What kind of time do you call this? We've been worried sick about you. That's it, no more going out with your friends – you are grounded until the end of term!'
say: 'You are an hour late, so you may not go out with your friends tomorrow. The next time you are given a time to be in, make sure you stick to it.'

Instead of: 'We don't want your kind in this club. Go away and don't come back.'

say: 'I'm giving you a one-week ban. If you're prepared to stick to the rules, you will be welcome back after that.'

Sanctions should be <u>limited in time</u>

Beware of punishing for something that has already been punished for elsewhere. I heard of a boy who was put on report at school. When his parents learnt of this, they were so angry that they grounded him for the whole of the Easter holiday. Instead of the boy returning from the holiday refreshed, able to move on and start the new term with a positive attitude, he returned resentful, convinced that the whole world was against him.

Telling someone's parents about their behaviour can in itself be a sanction.

The youth worker was trying to organise a game but no one was listening or co-operating, so she lost patience and said they wouldn't play the game after all. The teenagers thought this was unfair and one of them encouraged everyone to stage a sit-in. Everyone sat down and sang 'We shall not be moved'. The youth worker tried ignoring them, swept up round them at the end of the session and asked them to leave, but they would still not be moved. So she told them that she would have to phone their parents. That did the trick – they got up and left.

She spent the rest of the evening visiting and phoning parents explaining that if the youth club was to run, the leaders had to know that members would do as they were asked. The parents all spoke to their sons and daughters and the following week things were back to normal.

Young people need to be encouraged to be open and honest about what they get up to. If they receive heavy reprimands or sanctions when they tell us things, then they will stop telling us and we will not find out what is going on.

A boy tells you about the pranks he and his friends got up to on the school bus, which included writing on the seat and making fun of other pupils.

Instead of: rebuking him severely for being a vandal and a bully

try: explaining that what might seem like fun to him and his friends could be seen as vandalism and bullying, and say you want him to treat the bus and his fellow pupils with respect.

If behaviour worsens after a sanction, it is common to apply heavier and heavier sanctions. That results in alienation between adults and young people. When sanctions are not having the desired effect, it is time to take a different approach and open up communication between both parties to sort the problem out. See sections on 'Sorting Out Difficulties', p. 82, and 'Facing the Big Issues', p. 90.

- Ensure boundaries are reasonable and known

- Use positive language to reinforce them

- Apply them fairly and consistently

- Give sanctions that are consequences of behaviour and limited in time

- Keep communication channels open

Giving Instructions

A lot of teenagers don't like being told what to do. If it feels controlling they feel obliged to resist. If we give instructions in a way that does not seem controlling, young people are much more likely to co-operate.

Young people tend to co-operate with people they respect, and respect people who show respect to them. Adults can set themselves up to win by approaching young people in a respectful way.

Instead of: 'What do you think you're doing playing football here? You're going to damage something – go and play somewhere else!'

say: 'Hi there. Looks like you're having good game. I'm a bit worried about the ball hitting the cars or a window. Would you go and play in the park?'

When young people feel they are recognised and treated courteously, it is easy for them to do what they are asked.

It often seems difficult to get young people to listen; it's as though they are in a different reality to adults. In many respects this is true: their priorities are different and their attention is on other things, which sometimes include messaging friends, listening to music, or playing a computer game.

But if we want to give instructions, we must first have their attention. When talking to one person, get their attention by saying their name. When it is a group, use a generic.

'Good morning, guys.'

'OK, team.'

Keep it light and pleasant, but loud enough to get everyone's attention. If anyone has earphones in, they may have to take them out (sign language can help here). If they are at a computer, you may need them to look at you. Calling from a distance to someone on a computer can be a frustrating experience for both parties; it's often more effective to go and speak to them directly.

It often helps to give some warning.

'Dinner's nearly ready. I'll be asking you to lay the table in a minute.'

'There's a job needs doing. I need four volunteers please.'

'Five more minutes.'

Once you have their attention, give instructions as simply and clearly as possible. If they have done the task before, it can be a general instruction.

'Lay five places for dinner.'

'Put the bag in the locker.'

'Time to pack up.'

If more specific instructions are needed, they should be clear and unambiguous.

'There are five people. Each place needs a knife, fork and spoon and a glass.'

'Lift up the bag using the strap nearest you.'

'Put the small equipment on the shelves and the large equipment on the floor.'

The human brain isn't very good at distinguishing between 'do' and 'don't', so say what you do want rather than what you don't want.

Instead of: 'Don't be late.'
say: 'Make sure you're back by six.'

Instead of: 'Stop talking.'
say: 'Let's have quiet.'

Instead of: 'Don't forget your packed lunch.'
say: 'Remember your packed lunch.'

You are more likely to motivate teenagers if you focus on the positive.

Instead of: 'You can't leave until this mess is cleared up.'
say: 'As soon as this mess is cleared up you can go.'

Young people find it easier to co-operate when they don't feel judged. Specific advice is more helpful than judgment.

Instead of: *'You aren't putting enough effort in.'*

say: 'To get good results you need to put some time in every day.'

or: 'You'll find it easier to move that pool table if you jack it up a little more.'

With a little imagination on an adult's part, unpleasant, dull or 'uncool' activity can be reframed as exciting or challenging.

Instead of: *'You moan about there being no food in the house, and then can't be bothered to help me bring the shopping in from the car.'*

say: 'I reckon you guys could empty the boot in no time by carrying four bags each.'

or: 'Let's see if we can get all the shopping into the kitchen in three journeys.'

Some young people, particularly boys, find a large task or a lot of instructions overwhelming. They respond better if given a single task or instruction, followed by another one after the first is completed.

Instead of: *'The coursework is due in on 3rd March.'*

say: 'I want a plan for your coursework in on Friday.'

then later: 'You've all done your coursework plans. I'd like a first draft of section one on Friday week.'

Instead of: 'I said, "Clear the table"!'
say: 'Will you put the glasses on the top rack in the dishwasher, please.'
then: 'Thanks, now stack the plates and put them in the bottom rack.'

Instead of: 'I asked you to tidy your room!'
say: 'Start by taking everything off the floor.'
then: 'That looks better already. Now put the clean clothes away and the dirty ones in your wash bin.'
then: 'Looking good! Just shut each drawer and the job's done.'

People often ask whether instructions should be followed by 'please'. Young people need to hear the adults around them setting a good example, but if a respectful tone is used, the word 'please' may not be needed. Using 'thank you' with an instruction can help get co-operation, because it conveys confidence that the instruction will be carried out.

'Put everything away now. Thank you!'

- **Be respectful**

- **Get attention**

- **Be clear and concise**

- **Use positive language**

- **Give one instruction at a time**

Dealing with Questions

Used skilfully, questions can really help in communication with young people, but all too often the wrong question is used at the wrong time, and just makes a situation worse.

Take the example of a teacher whose questions escalated a minor problem out of all proportion:

Teacher: 'Where's your blazer?'

Boy: 'In my bag.'

Teacher: 'Why aren't you wearing it?'

Boy: 'Because I'm more comfortable without it.'

Teacher: 'And would you be comfortable having a lunchtime detention?'

Boy (shrugging): 'Maybe.'

Teacher: 'And would you be comfortable having an after school detention?'

Boy: 'No.'

Teacher: 'Well, you have a detention at lunchtime today and after school tomorrow and then we'll see how comfortable you are!'

Asking Questions

Before asking a question consider what you are trying to achieve and whether a question will help. Only ask a question if you actually need an answer.

Instead of: 'Where's your blazer?'

say: **'Put your blazer on please.'**

If you do ask a question, then acknowledge the answer in a way that will help achieve your objective.

Teacher: 'Where's your blazer?'

Boy: 'In my bag.'

Instead of: 'Why aren't you wearing it?'

say: **'OK. Would you put it on please.'**

Teacher: 'Where's your blazer?'

Boy: 'In my bag.'

Teacher: 'Why aren't you wearing it?'

Boy: 'Because I'm more comfortable without it.'

Instead of: 'And would you be comfortable having a lunchtime detention?'

say: **'Yes it's warm today, but you know the school rules so I'd like you to put it on please.'**

I'd recommend using *'would you'* when talking to boys and *'could you'* or *'can you'* when talking to girls. Boys often interpret 'could you' or 'can you' literally – as 'are you able' rather than 'will you'. They often say 'yes', then don't do anything; when you enquire why, they explain that you didn't actually ask them to do something, you asked whether they were able to.

Girls, on the other hand, usually respond well to 'could you' or 'can you' because they are less literal and more interested in creating a relationship; 'could you' or 'can you' is a gentle way of asking for their co-operation.

Only ask a question if you need an answer

Adults often ask questions in the hope of getting to the bottom of a misdemeanour, but this frequently provokes defensiveness and lying.

Question:	*Defensive Response:*
'Who did this?'	*'It wasn't me!'*
'What are you doing?'	*'Nothing.'*
'Why did you do that?'	*'Because I did.'*

Use a statement instead of a question.

Instead of: 'Who did this?'
say: 'I'd like this mess cleared up.'
or: 'I'd like whoever did this to be brave enough to own up.'

Instead of: 'Why did you do that?'
say: 'You know that the rule is x, so the sanction for doing this is y.'

Instead of: 'What kind of work do you call this?'
say: 'I feel really frustrated when I see someone of your ability do work like this.'

Questions of any sort tend to put people on the defensive, and adolescents can be particularly sensitive. It helps to preface a question with a sentence that shows your intention is positive, so they don't think you are being nosey or accusing.

Instead of: 'What are you doing?'

say: 'It sounds like you're having a good time. What are you doing?'

or: 'I don't think you should be in there. What are you doing?'

Instead of: 'How could you do something like that?'
say: 'It's not like you to do something like that. What's the matter?'

Instead of: 'How was your day?'
say: 'I had a pretty stressful day at work – I'm glad to be home. How was your day?'
or: 'You seem a bit low. Anything happen at school?'

If you want a truthful response, use a tone of voice that makes it clear that it is a sincere enquiry.

Teenagers are notorious for responding with grunts or minimal information, and parents are often frustrated when the child about whom they used to know everything becomes monosyllabic. But one thing is sure – asking teenagers lots of questions is a good way of shutting them down.

If you want to find out about what's going on in a young person's life, go about it gently, in an informal situation with no pressure: in the car or while you are doing something together can work well. Letting them play their music prevents them retreating behind headphones. Don't have a particular agenda; just let the conversation go where it leads. You could start by talking about the music.

'I quite liked that track. Who is it?'

'I didn't get the lyrics on that one. What are they saying?'

Or you might ask about things that they're interested in.

'How's your team doing?'

'Do you see much of Katie these days?'

Whether you get short answers or long ones, remember to acknowledge what they say so they know you are listening to them. Some young people will open up straight away, others may not, but if you get into the habit of regular conversation that does not involve telling them what to do or telling them off, they will be more willing to share parts of their life with you.

Adults who are teaching or coaching can use questions to assist learning, involve students, review an exercise or assess knowledge. You can check out how students are doing with questions such as:

'How did you find that exercise?'

'What did you learn from that?'

'How did you think that went?'

'How's it going so far?'

'How did you feel you did out there?'

'How could we improve that next time?'

These questions encourage reflection and will give you an insight into how the students are responding.

Do not ask questions that require reflection when there is a time constraint or the student is in mid-process, as this puts them under pressure and prevents clear thinking. In this situation they just need a brief instruction to remind them what to do.

Instead of: 'What did I tell you to do?'
say: 'Do x.'

When there is time for reflection, questions can be used to encourage self-assessment.

'What do you think you did well?'

'Are there any areas you want to improve?'

But if there is something specific you want someone to know, it is often better to give direct feedback (see p.60) than ask questions in the hope they will arrive at the 'right' conclusion.

Checking questions can be used to help get young people on side, gain agreement or find out their opinion.

'Are you with me so far?'

'Do you see what I mean?'

'Do you agree with this?'

'OK.?'

Listen and respond to whatever they say, especially if it's negative. It's better to find out what they are thinking than wrongly assume everyone is on board and then have problems later.

Answering Questions

Adults often make the mistake of reacting adversely to young people's questions instead of giving a straightforward answer.

Question: *'What position am I in?'*

Instead of: *'You should have been listening when I told everyone.'*

say: 'You're doing x.' / 'I'd like you over there.'

Question: *'Where's my jacket?'*

Instead of: *'Can't you look after any of your things? Do I have to do everything for you?'*

say: 'In your room.'

or: 'I don't know. Try your room.'

When young people ask to do things, it's easy to find yourself saying 'no' all the time. Rather than telling them what they can't do, try telling them what they can do.

Question: *'Can I sleepover at Sam's tonight?'*
Instead of: *'No.' / 'Not today.'*
say: **'I don't think it's a good idea on a school night, but it would be fine on Friday or Saturday.'**

Question: *'Can you buy me some new trainers?'*
Instead of: *'No.' / 'Not today.' / 'Have you any idea how broke I am at the moment?!'*
say: **'I will buy you a pair at the end of the holidays.'**
or: **'I'm prepared to contribute £25 towards a pair and would like you to pay the rest.'**

From around fifteen, teenagers can become fascinated by deep philosophical questions and are often very idealistic. Some develop an interest in religion or science; some have concerns about global issues; some question orthodox beliefs and practices; some experiment with unconventional belief systems.

Whilst younger children may need simple answers to such questions, teenagers need to explore them fully and come to their own conclusions, which they may later develop or change. Treat their views respectfully; listen and find out the thinking behind them; gently offer your own thoughts, beliefs and observations where appropriate.

'That's a really important question. Have you come up with any answers yet?'

'This is what I think. What do you think?'

'In my experience ...'

'I used to think .... Now I think ...'

'For me what's fundamental is ...'

Young people need a safe place to explore ideas, where they don't feel preached at or judged, and won't lose face if they later change their mind. If you can offer them that place, then you are providing a sanctuary that will serve them in good stead on their journey to adulthood.

- **Phrase questions carefully**

- **Acknowledge the answer you are given**

- **Preface a question with a statement that shows where you are coming from**

- **Respond to questions with short factual answers**

- **Allow young people to explore deeper questions**

Giving Feedback

Young people's self-image and behaviour are heavily influenced by the feedback they receive as they grow up.

When people feel liked, they believe themselves likeable; if they feel loved, they believe themselves lovable; if they experience success, they believe themselves capable. This sense of self in turn affects their behaviour: people who feel good about themselves usually behave well; people who feel bad about themselves often behave badly.

Labelling can start young, and youngsters who are constantly seen and described as, for example, 'trouble' or 'no-hopers' are likely to become what they have been labelled.

Most characteristics have both a positive and a negative side: someone who is outspoken tends to speak the truth, but can be insensitive to others' feelings; a ring-leader is able to harness the energies of their peers; skateboarders in urban areas might be viewed as unsociable and dangerous, or as skilful and brave.

The more adults see and feed back the best in young people, the more young people will develop that side of themselves.

Praise

Adults often give feedback through praise – 'Well done!', 'Fantastic!', 'You're a star!'. Most young people respond well to this and it makes them feel good. However, it doesn't give them a clear picture of themselves – what exactly was it that made them good, fantastic, or a star?

They can get a clearer picture if the feedback is more specific.

'I know I can rely on you to sort out the equipment properly and put it away.'

'You certainly know your way round a computer.'

'You do make me laugh!'

'It was brave of you to stand up to them.'

'Everyone worked hard to make that a success.'

The more specific you are, the more they will understand exactly what they are doing right.

'Thank you for stacking the dishes by the sink.'

'I've seen you practising all week. You're getting better every day.'

'You got down to your homework, then went out with your friends. It's great to see you taking charge of your life.'

'You being honest about breaking that window means we can sort it out without me getting angry.'

'I noticed you looking out for Jim. That was kind.'

'The team never let up on the attack even when it was clear we wouldn't be able to win.'

Being specific also helps avoid the burden of unrealistic expectations. Someone who is always being told they are clever may find it difficult when they don't understand; and someone who is frequently told they are a winner may take it badly when they lose.

Sometimes a young person's self-esteem is so low that praise is discounted.

Adult: 'You're really good at that.'
Young person: 'No I'm not, I'm rubbish!'

Being specific avoids such disagreement.

'I like the way the yellow blends into the green on your poster.'

'You balanced on the unicycle without holding on to anything. It takes most people ages before they can do that.'

Find a positive label for the behaviour you've witnessed.

*'You did all your homework without being reminded. It takes **self-discipline** to do that.'*

*'Thanks for giving up your seat. It's nice to know that **chivalry** is still alive today.'*

*'It was **courageous** to stick to your principles in that discussion even though your friends were giving you a hard time.'*

If you tell young people what you like about them, they will feel recognised and want to live up to this reputation. But sometimes there seems little to praise; you may have to look to the past to find something to comment on.

'Do you remember when you used to help out in the tuck shop? The younger kids really looked up to you.'

'Mrs Elwin said you used to walk her dog for her every week. She reckons you have a natural way with animals.'

Or you could describe the *nearest thing* to the behaviour you desire.

To someone who avoids helping in the house:
'Thanks for putting your clothes in the wash bin.'

To someone who is often late:
'You are five minutes earlier than yesterday.'

To someone who is often rude:
'I noticed how polite you were when the visitor came. I'm sure they felt welcome.'

When you do this, something unexpected usually happens – the young person moves in the direction you want, i.e. they become more helpful, punctual or polite.

This is an extremely powerful technique, and worth practising.

If describing what young people are doing right reinforces positive behaviour, does describing what they do wrong reinforce negative behaviour? It seems likely. To get the behaviour we want from young people – at home, at school, in the community and in society – adults need to notice and tell young people what they are doing right.

Go round catching young people doing things right!

Constructive Criticism

Young people also need feedback when they do things wrong. It should be phrased in a way they can take on board; otherwise it'll either make no difference or just make things worse.

Make it clear it is the *behaviour* you find unacceptable, not the person.

Instead of: 'How dare you be so insolent!'

say: 'The way you said that was very rude.'

Instead of: 'You're nothing but a bully. You should be ashamed of yourself!'

say: 'I like you Stephanie, but I don't like the way you treat your friends.'

**Criticise the <u>behaviour</u>
not the person**

What you describe is what you get more of, so *describe what you want* rather than what you don't want.

Instead of: 'That's a pack of lies. I can't trust anything you say!'

say: 'I want to trust you, so I need you to tell me the truth.'

Instead of: 'I don't want any divers on my team!'

say: 'Stay on your feet when you are tackled – it's harder for them to get the ball.'

Instead of: 'I don't expect you to be rude to your neighbours.'

say: 'I expect everyone on this street to be polite to their neighbours.'

As teenagers don't respond well to lectures, be specific and concise.

'I gave you money and didn't get any change.'

'Your room has clothes all over the floor.'

It is worth looking for the positive sides of the characteristics young people are displaying, and considering whether these can be encouraged.

'Your friends listen to what you say; you clearly have leadership qualities. You need to be careful what you encourage them to do.'

'I was disappointed you didn't tell me you'd be home late. But on reflection it's the first time for ages that you've not been on time. That makes you pretty reliable.'

There are some characteristics that are harder to see in a positive light than others, but these can be the ones most worth exploring. Someone who is rude to an adult might be *courageous* to have spoken out; someone who gets into fights might have a keen *sense of justice*; someone who is devious may be *clever*; someone who lies may be *imaginative* or have a strong *survival instinct*. This wider, more generous interpretation does not, of course, mean you condone bad behaviour.

'You've a very quick mind, but you haven't mastered tact yet. What you said was completely out of order.'

Sometimes young people need to hear about the effect they have on others.

Instead of: 'You left the place in such a state, you're not allowed out tonight!'

say: 'When I saw the state of the place, I was upset and disappointed.'

If young people feel blamed they will become defensive. Make the feedback factual so they are more likely to hear and learn from it.

Instead of: 'Your selfishness makes me really angry!'

say: 'When the phone bill comes in this high, I worry about how we're going to pay it.'

Give facts, not opinions

Make sure they understand the problem.

Instead of: 'Your attitude is bad.'

say: 'When you arrive late it gives the impression you're not serious.'

Reminding young people of times in the past when they displayed positive qualities can help, as long as this does not put them down.

To someone who is trying to get out of helping:

Instead of: 'You used to be such a helpful child; now you are just lazy and self-centred.'

say: 'I remember when you were eleven and you used
to help sweep up. You always wanted to mop the floor as
well and were really disappointed when I wouldn't let
you!'

Building Self-Esteem

Adolescence brings with it angst and self-doubt.
However confident teenagers may seem on the outside,
however brash or sophisticated, many are worried about
their looks, physique, ability, sexuality and their place
among their peers. Their apparent confidence can mask
turmoil inside.

If a young person has a poor self-image, then they are
unlikely to believe your praise unless it is based on facts.

Instead of: 'You look lovely in that outfit.'
  ['No, I don't, I'm fat and ugly!']
say: 'The colour of that outfit really suits you.'

Don't argue with their negative self-view; just build
evidence to the contrary.

On a boat, when teaching how to coil a rope:
Teenager: 'I'm useless at this, ask someone else to do it!'
Instead of: 'You're not useless!'
  ['Yes I am!']
  or: 'It's quite easy, I'll show you.'
  ['If it's easy, I must be useless!']

> *or: 'Everyone else has had a turn.'*
> >   *['Not me!']*

say: 'It is quite tricky. Watch how I do it. Now you try.'

then: 'Yes that's right, make sure the coils are about the same size.'

then: 'You're getting the hang of this.'

then: 'Perfect!'

You can help build a positive self-image by describing to a young person the positive things they have done.

'I know you found that hard, but you tried it anyway. I admire that.'

And then put a positive label on what you describe.

'It was brave of you to admit that you did that.'

'You kept screwing up your drawings until you were completely satisfied with one. I can see you're a bit of a perfectionist!'

It can help to refer to something they did well.

To someone who doesn't want to try a new activity:

'Remember when you were learning to rollerblade? Even though you kept falling over, you kept on practising. Then all of a sudden it clicked!'

When people operate below their potential, it is easy to dwell on what they are *not* doing rather than on the potential you see. The result is self-fulfilling: a girl who is told she is lazy switches off and does nothing; a boy who is told he is clumsy becomes self-conscious and uncomfortable in his body. Hold up a picture of them at their best, then subtly invite them to live up to it.

To someone with a rarely used artistic ability:

'We need some posters to advertise the event. Will you design one for us?'

To someone with a mechanical bent:

'I can't get anyone to mend this. Would you have a look at it for me?'

If you demonstrate your confidence in them, teenagers often live up to it.

To someone who isn't trying at school:

'I think you could do very well in this subject.'

To someone who gets ready at the last minute:

'I know you like to be on time, so why don't you get your things ready five minutes before you need to leave.'

To teenagers in the park:

'I'm sure you'll keep an eye out for the younger ones and make sure no one gets hurt.'

By treating young people as though they already have the characteristics we desire in them, we help shape them into the people we want them to become.

> • **Speak to the best in a young person**
>
> • **Focus on the positive**
>
> • **Give facts, not judgements**
>
> • **Acknowledge steps in the right direction**
>
> • **Catch young people doing things right**

Expressing Feelings

Adolescence is an emotional time. With hormones racing it's all too easy for feelings to get out of control. Adults can help by recognising and containing young people's feelings, and not letting their own feelings add fuel to the fire.

Their Feelings

Teenagers are a bundle of emotions. While they tend not to share their feelings with adults, we still feel the brunt of the emotional rollercoaster they are riding. Talking about feelings without prying into their personal life may help them through this ride.

'The more nervous you are about something, the more courage it takes to do it.'

'I bet you're proud of yourself!'

'Well done for overcoming your embarrassment and asking them again.'

Acknowledging emotions allows young people to accept them and move on. They don't need you to fix their problems, but it can help to know someone understands how they feel.

To someone who has not been picked for a position:
'You must be disappointed not to be chosen.'

To someone having trouble with a computer:

'Computers can be so frustrating when they don't do what you want.'

Don't worry if you put the wrong label on the emotion; you will soon be put right.

Adult: 'You must be really upset about your friends not showing up.'

Teenager: 'I'm not upset, I'm angry! They all promised me they'd come.'

Your empathy can help them recognise their true feelings.

Adult: 'If it was me I'd be quite frightened of moving to a different part of the country.'

Teenager: 'Frightened? I'm terrified!'

Whilst any feeling can be accepted, certain behaviours must be limited.

'I can see you are angry about this, but try to talk about it without swearing.'

Aggression can mask deeper emotions

Anger or sullenness may be masking emotions such as inadequacy, humiliation, rejection or fear. Be sensitive to this.

Instead of: '*Just because you aren't in the team, you don't have to take it out on everyone else!*'

say (privately): 'Are you upset not to be in the team?'

Try to acknowledge the underlying emotion.

To someone who vandalises a club after being banned from it:

'You must have been feeling really hurt to want to do that.'

Questions can help check how young people are feeling.

'Are you missing your friends?'

'Does it feel like no one is listening to you?'

'Are you disappointed that you're not going?'

'Do you feel like you're being controlled?'

Sometimes young people deal with fear, pressure or feelings of inadequacy by avoidance. Apparent laziness might mask a sense of being overwhelmed.

Instead of: '*You won't get decent grades if you never do any work for your exams!*'

say: 'Are you feeling under pressure with the exams coming up?'

At some point teenagers are likely to experience falling in love, jealousy or rejection. Mood swings may not only be caused by hormone levels, but also by a young person's love life. Make some allowances for this.

Instead of: 'Will you answer when you're spoken to!'
[She does, with some very choice language.]
say: 'You're not your usual self – is anything up?'

While young people are unlikely to want to go into detail, they might nonetheless appreciate some empathy.

Adult: 'How's Megan?'

Boy: 'We're not going out.'

Adult: 'Oh. I thought you really liked her.'

Boy: 'She dumped me.'

Adult: 'That must really hurt.'

Boy: 'It does.'

An empathetic approach shows that you are there if they need you.

Your Feelings

When young people's behaviour seems unreasonable, adults' emotions can also run high. Mix this with the untutored emotions of youth and you have a lethal cocktail. However unreasonable teenagers may seem, we must remember that we are the adults, and it is from us that they will learn how to deal with their emotions responsibly – we have to set the example. The first step is to put our feelings into words.

A teenage boy had been asked to clear away after dinner; it was one of his regular household chores. Some time later his father saw the dishes still on the table and yelled angrily at the boy to get the job done. His son shouted back. The father paused, then said: 'To tell you the truth, I'm not so much angry that you didn't do it, as disappointed that after all this time we still have to remind you to do your job.'
The boy cleared up without further comment.

Some people worry that expressing how they feel will make things worse and create an atmosphere. This certainly can happen, and it's sometimes wisest to say nothing. But an atmosphere can also be created by what is left *unsaid*. Stating what you think and feel can clear the atmosphere and allow everyone to move on.

Explosions caused by bottled-up emotions can be avoided by expressing how you feel at the time.

'I'm getting irritated by the level of noise.'

'Seeing all this mess makes me really angry.'

'I was so embarrassed just now when I showed the visitor round and heard you swearing.'

It is important that we as adults take responsibility for our own feelings and don't leave young people feeling blamed for them, as blame causes resentment.

> *Instead of:* *'You make me feel ...'*
> *say:* *'When you do ... I feel ...'*

Instead of: *'You make me furious – you never listen to anything I say!'*
say: *'When you ignore what I say, I feel angry.'*

Instead of: *feeling taken for granted*
or saying: *'You take me for granted.'*
say: *'When I don't get a thank-you, I feel taken for granted.'*

Telling anecdotes about how you deal with your own feelings shows young people how they might deal with theirs:

'You know, I dread sorting out the attic. I've decided that instead of tackling the whole job at once I'll do one bit at a time.'

'That's the fifth night running the neighbours' car alarm has gone off. I was steaming, and nearly went round at 3.00 a.m. to tell them exactly what I thought of them. But I realised I'd probably say something I'd regret, and decided to wait till the morning when I'd had time to calm down and think about what to say.'

Young people will also learn from you talking about other people's feelings:

'Granny was really upset that you wouldn't do as she asked.'

'Do you think he felt scared when he did that?'

'He must have been devastated when he missed that penalty!'

It is important that the emotions described are real; otherwise young people won't take them seriously or will feel manipulated.

Say how you feel, then move on

Depression

Everyone feels low from time to time, and teenagers need to learn how to cope with life's ups and downs. However, a mood that is out of character and goes on for weeks may turn into depression, resulting in a lack of motivation and feelings of hopelessness.

Depression can be brought on by major changes such as moving house or school, bereavement, divorce, or a new step-parent; by worries about relationships, appearance, sexuality, or money; or by pressure from peers, parents or school.

Symptoms of depression in young people are:

- drop in school performance
- social withdrawal at home or at school
- insomnia or excessive sleep
- lack of concentration / poor memory
- stomach aches / headaches / feeling sick
- apathy / fatigue
- loss or increase in appetite
- aggression
- drug or alcohol abuse

If you suspect depression, seek help. If untreated, clinical depression can last for several months or even years, and is associated with a risk of suicide.

Ask the advice of your doctor, who may be able to refer the young person to a counsellor. There may also be a counselling service in their school or college. This is a time when you may need to push your teenager gently but firmly to seek and receive help.

- Acknowledge young people's feelings

- Talk about your own and others' feelings

- Take responsibility for your own feelings

- Any feeling can be accepted; certain behaviours must be limited

How to Stop Nagging and Shouting

Nobody likes being nagged or shouted at, and young people often respond by tuning out the adult who is doing it.

Part of an adult's job is to train up the next generation; but they won't always remember to do what you ask them and they will need frequent reminding. We have to take care that reminding does not turn into nagging and then, with frustration, develop into shouting.

To avoid nagging and shouting:

> • **Limit what you say**
> • **Keep it positive**

Use a gesture

The best way to limit what you say is to say nothing at all.

You want someone to be quiet:
put a finger to your lips, or 'zip' your lips.

Someone comes in with dirty trainers:
point to them and make a grimace.

Someone is sitting on the table:
gesture getting off it.

A rule is being broken:
point to the notice where that rule is written.

Making the gesture humorous often helps. I met a teacher working in a special unit for teenagers who used to hold her nose when she thought she smelled 'bullshit'. The students laughed, but knew they had been caught out.

Say it in a word

They often forget their lunch,
say: 'Lunchbox.'

They are chewing where gum is not allowed,
say: 'Gum.'

It's time to do homework,
say: 'Homework.'

The seatbelt is undone,
say: 'Seatbelt.'

Give information

Be clear and factual.

Instead of: 'This room is like a pigsty! Come and clear it up right this minute!'
say: 'The clothes on the floor need to be put away.'

Instead of: 'Who left this mess in the kitchen?'
say: 'Whoever used the kitchen needs to clean it up.'

Instead of: 'Late again!'

say: 'This is the second time you've been late this week.'

Instead of: 'Why haven't you done your homework?'
say: 'That homework is due in tomorrow.'

Describing what you see or hear may be enough.

Instead of: 'Right, that's it! I let you have a sleepover and you keep everyone awake with your noise. Don't expect to have one again!'

say: 'I can hear your music from my room.'

State positive expectations

When expectations are not being met, it is helpful to restate them.

Instead of: 'Look at the state of this room!'
say: 'I expect you to clean up after yourself.

Instead of: 'I can't believe how lazy and ungrateful you lot are!'

say: 'I expect everyone to help put the equipment away after it has been used.'

Instead of: 'What do I have to do to get you to come in on time?'

say: 'When we agree a time, I expect you to honour it.'

Restating rules will remind young people of your expectations.

Instead of: *'How dare you use language like that!'*
say: **'We have a "no swearing" rule here.'**

Say what needs to be done

Focus on the solution rather than the problem.

Instead of: *'I'm sick of having to tell you to do your homework. Don't think you'll be going out with your friends today!'*
say: **'As soon as you've finished your homework you can go and see your friends.'**

Instead of: *'Stop kicking that ball so high; you're going to break something!'*
say: **'Keep the ball low.'**

Put it in writing

The written word can be very effective. It gives adults time to think about what needs to be said and the young people space for consideration.

A sign by the door:
Leave dirty trainers outside.

A reminder on the board before an outing:
Meet in the car park tomorrow at 9.00 a.m.
Bring a packed lunch and a jacket.

A notice in the park:
Put litter in the bin. Thanks.

A note on the bed:
I am washing tomorrow. Put your dirty clothes in the wash bin before you go to bed. xxx

---

- Use a gesture

- Say it in a word

- Give information

- State expectations

- Say what needs to be done

- Put it in writing

Avoiding Conflict and Arguments

Sometimes communication with teenagers escalates to conflict. It takes two for this to happen, and if an adult is involved, we are the ones who should have the skills and maturity to avoid it or to de-escalate the situation.

As young people's bodies develop into that of an adult, they want to be treated more like one; when they feel they aren't, they fight for recognition. If the adult perceives this as a threat to his or her authority and attempts to keep them in their place, an unhealthy competition emerges, resulting in confrontation and argument; sometimes this gets physical.

Adults can avoid these head-on collisions by adopting a non-confrontational approach.

Instead of: 'If you want to be treated like an adult, you need to behave like one!'

say: 'Yes, it is time you were treated like an adult. Maybe we should discuss what that involves.'

Challenging young people in a confrontational way frequently provokes challenging behaviour; a non-confrontational approach is likely to get a more positive response.

Instead of: 'Stop that bloody noise or I'll call the police!'

say: 'I can hear you from the other end of the street –
will you turn the noise down.'

If you back someone into a corner, they normally react by fighting back, partly because they feel trapped and partly because they don't want to lose face. Allow young people to save face by giving them an honourable way out.

Instead of: humiliating them in front of others
whisper: 'I saw that.'

Instead of: insisting on a particular course of action
offer choices: 'Do you want to repair the damage or pay for someone else to?'
or: 'I think that requires an apology. Have a think whether you'd rather apologise to them face to face or write a letter.'

Instead of: being controlling or heavy about an issue
use humour: 'The next person who comes in here with muddy shoes will find themselves walking on their hands!'

> **Give teenagers an honourable way out**

Some youngsters actively seek conflict because they enjoy the buzz it gives them. Don't fall into the trap of letting them wind you up and giving them the fight they are looking for.

When things go wrong, try 'rewinding' then replaying the scene in a different way.

A girl comes in late and you confront her. She loses it and swears at you.

say: 'Neither of us did that very well. I think we need to rewind. Why don't you go out, come back in and I'll try again.'

Once they understand the technique, young people may use it themselves.

'Sorry, I didn't mean to be rude. I'm going to rewind.'
You can have a similar effect using 'cut' and 'take two'.

When things get heated, it's easy to say or do things that you later regret. Take a few seconds to step back and think before doing or saying anything. Those few seconds may make the difference between conflict and co-operation.

If you do overstep the mark, then be big enough to apologise. This will not only de-escalate the situation, but also set a good example.

You can also de-escalate a situation by acknowledging what the teenager is saying.

Teenager: 'You can't tell me what to do – you're not my dad!'

Adult: 'No, I'm not your dad. But I would like you to be respectful in the house.'

It's good policy not to bring up the past. Just deal with the issues that face you in the present.

Instead of: 'I wish we hadn't brought you – you always spoil everything! Last time you ruined the trip to the cinema and now you're messing up the bowling.'

say: 'Put the bowls down until it's your turn.'

Don't be tempted to make comparisons.

Instead of: 'Your brother didn't need me to be on his case about homework the whole time. Why can't you follow his example?'

say: 'I'm getting frustrated having to remind you about your homework. Let's sit down and work out a way you can get it done without me nagging you to death!'

If a teenager is under the influence of drugs or alcohol, they can be more sensitive to a perceived slight and become quite aggressive. Avoid conflict by being friendly and firm.

When there is a lot of conflict in a household, sometimes parents reach the end of their tether and tell a teenager to move out. This usually happens when emotions are running high on both sides; it is not the time to make such an important decision.

Wait until everyone has calmed down before making important decisions

---

Young people need to live in a place that provides the support they require until they are mature enough to leave home. To get this support they may occasionally need to move from one home to another, particularly if their parents are separated. If a young person does need to move, this should be done after reflection, discussion and planning, with a trial period and a time to review the situation.

Being respectful to young people does not mean tolerating disrespect from them, but it does mean addressing disrespectful behaviour in a respectful way:

Instead of: 'How dare you use that language in front of my children!'

say: 'My kids are a bit young to hear that kind of language, and to be honest I don't like it either. I'd appreciate it if you didn't swear when we can hear you. Would you do that for me?'

The more young people experience non-confrontational approaches for preventing and resolving conflict, the more they will be able to adopt those approaches and take them into their adult lives.

- **Respond to challenging behaviour in a non-confrontational way**

- **Give young people an honourable way out**

- **Acknowledge feelings on both sides**

- **When things go wrong, 'rewind'**

- **Be big enough to apologise when necessary**

- **Do not dwell on the past**

PART III

Problem Solving

Sorting Out Difficulties

When you've tried every communication strategy you can think of and things still aren't working, take some time to work out how to address the problem, perhaps with the help of other adults or with the young people concerned.

Look for the cause of the behaviour and see if this can be addressed.

Problem: Boys won't help set up and clear up at youth club.

Reason: As soon as the balls are out they play football instead.

Solution: Give the balls out last and collect them in first.

Problem: Young people are regularly gathering outside an old people's home.

Reason: A clear piece of grass makes it a good place to play games and hang out.

Solution: Plant a rose garden in the space.

Problem: A girl is spending lots of time in her room and is disengaging from the family.

Reason: She is using her computer for social networking.

Solution: Have regular family meals together; choose DVDs for family viewing; put a timer switch on the wireless router.

If you look for the possible *motive* behind young people's behaviour, it might give you an insight into how to *motivate* them.

If they don't like being told what to do, they probably want some control over their life; giving them some decision-making power might make them more co-operative.

If they don't want to try new experiences, they may be afraid of failure; pointing out what they are good at may give them the confidence to try new things.

If they boast a lot, they might want reassurance that they are good enough; some unsolicited words of praise might provide that reassurance.

Attention Seeking

Many people find attention-seeking behaviour very irritating and often respond by trying to ignore it. Sometimes this works; at other times it just makes it worse.

Consider what might be behind the behaviour. It might be that the person concerned literally wants, and perhaps needs, your attention. Giving them attention might solve the problem.

But sometimes giving attention merely encourages further irritating behaviour, so give them attention *before* they start demanding it. When they realise they can have the attention they seek, they will gradually stop the attention-seeking behaviour.

Whilst attention seeking is annoying, it does have a positive side: at some level, the young person is aware of his or her needs and is seeking to fulfil these. It would be much worse if they were unaware of their needs, and instead became withdrawn or depressed.

Win-Win Negotiation

We often talk about winning and losing arguments, but it is possible to reach agreements with both parties satisfied. To negotiate a win-win agreement with young people, you have first to listen carefully to their point of view and seek to understand it. Only when they feel you have understood them will they be prepared to listen to your point of view. Once listening has taken place, finding a mutually agreeable solution is relatively easy.

- Listen to their point of view
- Acknowledge their point of view
- Describe your point of view
- Explore options
- Find areas of agreement

Teenager's point of view: Everyone else is allowed out till midnight. You don't trust me. You are controlling. You treat me like a kid.

Parent's acknowledgement: 'I know you want to stay out late like some of your friends. I can see that me wanting you in earlier might seem controlling, and I

understand that you want to be trusted and treated more like an adult.'

Parent's view: 'When you are out late I worry about your safety. I'm also concerned about your school work; this is your exam year and if you are over-tired you won't do as well as you could.'

After talking about it they agree that on Fridays and Saturdays during term-time the teenager can stay out till 11 p.m. and during holidays until midnight.

Making Contracts

In order for things to work, there need to be rules and/or agreements that will be kept. Where these aren't already in place, they need to be agreed upon, and if they aren't being kept they need to be revisited and new agreements made. One way of doing this is by making a 'contract'.

- Gather the young people together
- Tell them the objective / problem to solve
- Ask what agreements would achieve this
- Write down what everyone says
- Ask if these will achieve the objective
- Add or amend until they do
- Ask each individual if they are prepared to stick to these agreements
- Get everyone involved to sign their names
- Display it prominently

Brainstorming

When a problem is recurring or seems to be intractable, then a workable solution can be found by brainstorming with the young people concerned.

- Choose a time when emotions have subsided
- Write a simple description of the problem
- Think of as many solutions as possible
- Write down all suggested solutions to the problem; adults add ideas too
- No comments can be made until all ideas are written down
- Assess them together; if anyone disagrees with an idea, cross it out; if everyone agrees with it, tick it
- It's fine to add extra ideas or adapt ideas at this stage
- Talk through the ideas until you agree on a way to solve the problem
- Display it prominently

Now Josh was a teenager, he thought he was too old to have a bedtime. There were arguments every night. Once in bed it was a long time before he fell asleep. He was grumpy and unco-operative in the morning. Every five or six weeks he got a cold or a cough and stayed off school. Josh wanted to be in charge of his own life and didn't see the point of going to bed if he couldn't sleep. The parents thought the lack of sleep was affecting his mood, his learning and his health.

*The three of them sat down to brainstorm the problem
and eventually agreed on a plan.*
*Josh would be allowed to put himself to bed when he
liked as long as these conditions were kept:*
- His homework was done by 8.30 p.m.
- His TV and computer were off by 9.30 p.m.
*- No one else could hear any noise from him after they
   went to bed.*
*- He got himself up in the morning and went to school
   without any fuss.*
- He did not miss school through illness.
*If any of these conditions were not met, then for the next
three days Josh would have to be in his room by 9.00 p.m.,
with lights out by 9.30.*

Restorative Justice

Restorative justice is a method of sorting out problems
where one party is the victim and another the perpetrator.
It usually takes the form of a conversation between the
people involved and an independent third party.

During the conversation the perpetrator explains why
they did what they did, the victim and others describe the
impact it had on them, and then suggestions are made as
to what actions the perpetrator can take to make amends.
These are discussed and a plan is agreed.

If one or other of the parties do not want to meet, then a
similar process can take place through a mediator.

These are the kind of questions that are asked.

To the perpetrator:

'What happened?'
'What were you thinking about at the time?'
'What have you thought about since then?'
'Who do you think has been affected?'
'How have they been affected?'

To the victim:

'What was your reaction at the time?'
'How did you feel about what happened?'
'What was the hardest thing for you?'
'What would you like from this meeting?'

Such conversations allow the perpetrator to understand the full impact of their actions, and give the victim an opportunity to understand the background to the incident, to express their feelings directly to the perpetrator, and to ask for appropriate recompense. This might involve an apology; repairing, replacing or paying for damage; or some form of work for the victim or in the community.

- Look for the reason or motive behind behaviour

- Take time out to solve problems together

- Listen to everyone's point of view

- Seek areas of agreement

Facing the Big Issues

Teenagers desperately need opportunities to discuss the issues that affect them. If they feel the adults around them will judge or lecture them, then they will restrict such discussions to their peer group. Conversations with adults may give them different perspectives that will develop their thinking and may alter their views.

Use what is going on around you to open up discussions. The topic might be behaviour, facilities, or the community; health, exercise, or cigarettes; personal safety or gun and knife crime. The point is to explore the issue, not to reach a particular conclusion. You might start the conversation with an enquiry.

'There's something I don't understand. Can you explain it to me?'

'Did you hear about that stabbing last night? What do you think was going on there?'

Let people say what they think; allow others to disagree; make sure everyone listens to each other. Use questions to go deeper. Just having the conversation will encourage thinking and the development of views.

Alcohol

Most teenagers are likely to experiment with forbidden substances at some point: for some it will just be alcohol and cigarettes; for others it may involve harder drugs.

Parents can reduce the allure of alcohol and teach teenagers to approach drinking responsibly by allowing them moderate amounts of alcohol in the home – for example, with a weekend meal.

Conversations that teenagers often have about drinking can be broadened to explore the safety issues around alcohol, such as drink driving, binge drinking, alcohol-fuelled violence, and the dangers of sex when drunk.

'I heard that the boy who died in the car crash was over the limit.'

'What worries me when girls gets paralytic is that they become an easy target for someone.'

Drugs

Conversations about drugs need to be a two-way dialogue, seeking young people's views and telling them yours. To teenagers, adults who warn them off drugs can seem hypocritical if they have taken drugs themselves, or ignorant if they have no experience of drugs. Be prepared to acknowledge this, and explain the facts and reasons for your current views. Do not pretend to know anything you don't; rather, ask young people what they know, and suggest both of you seek further information.

Teenagers are subject to a lot of peer pressure when it comes to drugs; many will try them at some stage and most will come out the other side relatively unscathed. But, since the maturation of the brain is not complete until late teens or early twenties, prolonged use of drugs in adolescence can be more damaging than in adulthood, and can increase the likelihood of later addiction or depression.

> **Adults can help young people by:**
> - **making it clear they do not condone drugs**
> - **regularly talking about the issues**
> - **keeping abreast of information about drugs**
> - **staying in touch with other adults**

Sex

Teenagers can get a lot of misinformation about sex from their peers, so it is vital that adults give useful facts and guidance.

Rather than waiting for the 'right moment' to have a serious talk, adults can pick up on comments or jokes made about sex, and use the opportunity to check out understanding and give additional information or insights.

The use of the word 'gay' to insult a friend could prompt a discussion about sexuality. If sexual banter implies that everyone is sexually active, you could point out that there's often a disparity between what people say about sex and what's actually happening. If the language or concepts become disrespectful, explain the difference between joking and comments that degrade others.

Teenagers don't want to hear dire warnings about under-age sex, sexually transmitted diseases and teenage pregnancy, but these do need to be discussed so they have some reality about them.

See if you can get an idea of whether young people are sexually active and whether they use protection. Talk to them about what kind of relationships they want, what age they would like to have children and what kind of life they want their children to have. Check out whether the choices they are making are in line with what they say they want.

Teenagers need to learn about relationships

It is important for young people to learn about relationships and how to deal with their feelings. Adults might reassure young people with stories of their younger days, and also offer insights into the minds of the opposite sex.

Make it clear that all relationships go through difficult patches, and that part of what makes a successful relationship is working these through. By discussing relationships around you, including those portrayed in soaps, you can talk about acceptable and unacceptable behaviour, when it's worth sticking in a relationship and when it's time to leave.

It can be valuable to discuss the effect of parents' behaviour on children; all young people have a personal experience of this.

You may find it helps to share some of your experiences, but do not go into the details: disclosing too much information might compromise you or others, and in any case most young people prefer not to know details of adult relationships!

Sometimes young people intrude with their questions or comments. If a question is too personal, then make the boundaries clear; for example, that you are happy to give information, but not to discuss your private life.

- Keep communication channels open

- Share views and experiences but don't lecture

- Pick up on comments in young people's conversation

- Acknowledge your ignorance of certain areas

- Stay in touch with other adults about issues

Teenagers in the Community

When young people feel part of their local community, they show respect towards it and the people in it. If the adults in that community know them and are looking out for them, they feel safe and are less likely to cause problems.

In some communities teenagers are perceived as a nuisance or a threat, particularly if they hang out on the street. Sometimes this perception is justified; often it is not.

If the only time we talk to teenagers is to tell them off, we will get a negative reaction; if we cross the road to avoid them, then the streets become theirs.

If they are to feel part of the community, we need to engage positively with them – preferably well before any problems arise.

> **Engage with teenagers in the community**

When you are in a community for any length of time, you watch children grow up, become teenagers, sometimes cause problems, and then more often than not mature into responsible young adults.

You can help get them through the tricky teenage patch by creating a sense of community around them as they grow up.

The first thing to do is to get to know local people – neighbours, parents, young people and children. Pass the time of day with them, if necessary talk about the weather!

Get to know young people and their parents

Make a point of talking about what is working. Notice what young people are doing right and point it out to others, including their parents.

'I see Matt walks Mrs Gupta's dog every day now that she can't get out herself.'

When people are aware that things generally are going right, it is easier to keep things in proportion when they go wrong.

Build an informal network of adults interested in the community. Tell each other what's going on; seek their opinion if you have concerns; ask for their help when problems arise.

Include the police in your network, and encourage informal contact between young people and local police.

But do your best to avoid the police getting involved in minor incidents that can be resolved within the community. Young people should know that when the police are called in, it is serious.

Look for ways the generations can interact and get to know each another. Adults could pass on skills like crafts or bike maintenance; young people could earn money by washing cars, mowing lawns or doing odd jobs.

Encourage young people to put back into the community – by visiting old folk, helping at a club or organising fund-raising events.

Provide an extended family for youngsters who are having problems at home. If families in the community look out for everyone's children, they help those going through difficult patches come through the other side.

Form a good relationship with parents, so you can tactfully tip them off about what their children are up to. Young people will become aware of the network of adults and be more cautious about what they do. Sometimes you may choose not to tell parents about behaviour, but make it clear to the young people that you know what they are doing, and that if they carry on, their parents will know.

When teenagers are brought up in a community that interacts with them in a positive way, they grow into adults who in turn become role models for the next generation.

- Get to know local parents and their children

- Talk about the positive things that happen

- Build a network of interested adults

- Form a good relationship with local police

- Involve young people in community activities

- Sort out minor issues without police involvement

Summary

Bringing Out the Best in Teenagers

Understand their World

- See things through a teenager's eyes
- Talk to them and listen to their view of the world
- Acknowledge their reality and how they feel

Build Positive Relationships

- Assume the best in young people
- Don't over-react to teenagers' over-reactions
- Use humour to lighten the atmosphere
- Don't take young people's joking personally

Boundaries and Sanctions

- Set clear boundaries
- Apply rules fairly and consistently
- Choose sanctions that mirror behaviour
- Give sanctions that are limited in time
- Keep communication channels open

© Lucinda Neall

How to Get Co-operation

- Get their attention
- Say what needs to be done
- Use positive language
- Be clear, calm and concise

How to Avoid Conflict

- Respond to challenging behaviour in a non-confrontational way
- Only ask questions that need answers
- Give facts, not judgments
- When things go wrong, 'rewind'
- Do not dwell on the past
- Give young people an honourable way out

Catch teenagers doing things right!

---

howtotalktoteenagers.com

Acknowledgements

Thanks go to John Conway for the idea of this book, and John Scaife for galvanising me into action and giving valuable feedback. Also to my parents for providing a sanctuary in which to write, and to my husband, Peter, for being the first to read and comment on each draft. Thanks to Chris Baker, Luke Del Greco, Jane Higham, Phil Hood and Rory MccGwire for their comments and encouragement, to Deborah Hawkins for setting me up to win, and to Jeremy Mumford for the final polish.

I would also like to acknowledge some of the authors whose writings have influenced me over the years: Adele Faber & Elaine Mazlisch – *How to Talk so Kids will Listen*; Kenneth Blanchard & Spencer Johnson – *One Minute Manager*; John Gray – *Men are from Mars, Women are from Venus*; Marshall Rosenberg – *Non-Violent Communication*; Allan Pease – *Body Language*; Roger Fisher & William Ury – *Getting to a Yes*.

About the Author

LUCINDA NEALL has spent much of her working life training and coaching adults in motivation and communication. Since the publication of her two books on bringing the best out in boys, she has worked with teachers, parents and youth workers on setting boys up to succeed. She also provides courses for teenagers on probation and for ex-offenders, which help them look at who they are, where they have been and take steps to build a better future.

Over the years Lucinda has spent a lot of her spare time with young people, as a mother and stepmother, and on projects with teenagers in the community. She set up a youth forum, a music festival, a youth drama group, a community action group, and runs her local youth club. She feels passionately that local people can make a big difference.

Lucinda is also a volunteer watch leader for the Ocean Youth Trust.

If you would like to make any comments about the book or have Lucinda Neall address a group about talking to teenagers, please contact her at:

> lucinda@neallscott.co.uk
> 0044 (0) 1525 222 600
> www.howtotalktoteenagers.com

Copies of *How to Talk to Teenagers*, and Lucinda Neall's other two books, *About Our Boys* and *Bringing the Best Out in Boys – Communication Strategies for Teachers,* can be obtained online, from any good bookshop or ordered through your local library.